HERO-SURFING

by Anne Sheldon

For my cousin Luci; with love from Anne + Jamie

Washington Writers' Publishing House
Washington, DC

Grateful acknowledgement is made to the editors of the following journals in which these poems first appeared: *Antietam Review*, "After the First Ice Storm," "Auditions for 'Hamlet' at the Unitarian Church," and "Overheard on the Richmond Floodwall;" *The Dark Horse*, "Epiphany;" "Gertrude Lane Newberry," *Edge City Review*, "Eurydice;" *Heliotrope*, "Hero-surfing;" *The Living Church*, "The Common Cup;" *Metropolitain*, "If You Lived Here, You'd Be Home By Now;" *Painted Hills Review*, "Valentine's Night;" *Pivot*, "The Prince Who Woke Briar Rose;" *Poet Lore*, "March 11, 1421: Catherine of Valois," and "June 2, 1430: Catherine of Valois;" *Visions*, "Seneca Forest;" and *Weird Tales*, "Snow White Turns 39." I also give thanks to Word Works and Mica Press for bringing out my first chapbook, *Lancastrian Letters*.

Heartfelt thanks to all my writing friends who read these poems with interest and nudged them along, especially James Griffin, Jim Henley, Vicki Lambert, Nancy Jane Moore, Fred Pollack, Michael Schaffner, Peggy Weaver, and Matt Westbrook; and to all those at WWPH who helped me bring this book into being, especially Sid Gold, Bernie Jankowski, Jean Nordhaus, and most especially to Martin Galvin, my manuscript editor.

Portrait of Henry Sheldon by Marian Newberry Sheldon.
Cover art and design by Bernie Jankowski.
Production and layout by Bernie Jankowski.

Publication of this book is possible thanks to donations from the many Friends of Washington Writers' Publishing House.

Anne Sheldon, 1945-
Hero-surfing/ by Anne Sheldon
p. cm.
ISBN 0-931846-63-3 (alk. paper)
I. Title

PS3619.H453 H47 2002
813'.6--dc21

2002033185

Washington Writers' Publishing House
P.O. Box 15271
Washington, D.C. 20003

In memory of my father,
Henry Davidson Sheldon, Jr., 1904 —1976:
writer, reader, ukele player, gardener.

CONTENTS

HOW I MISS THE WOODSMAN

AFTER THE FOURTH ICE STORM

A bird could walk the crust but no bird does.
Another coat of glass will break the yew.
Nothing here remembers what it was.

Not even starlings at the feeder because
warmth, by now, is all that will renew.
A bird could walk the crust but no bird does.

Under the eaves, they must be ravenous.
We've forgotten that the sky was blue.
Nothing here remembers what it was.

Do you remember how it was for us?
Some must die, as all this cold accrues.
A bird could walk the crust but no bird does.

Living through the winter's dangerous.
I know the midnight phone call was for you.
Nothing here remembers what it was.

Every path and stone is treacherous.
Why must I imagine we'll come through.
A bird could walk the crust but no bird does.
Nothing here remembers what it was.

SENECA FOREST

Between river and lake the trail forgets,
gives way to honeysuckle brush and saplings.
We make the silence crackle underfoot,
the woods erupt and we see nothing but
we hear the quail, the bear. I find the hoofed
and whitened legbone of a deer.

Nodding to herself at water's edge
the bottle gentian is blue. Picking it,
I break the law, imagine it's the last
in West Virginia, and myself small,
small, inside the petals, lapis daylight
streaming in. I close my eyelids

but the room inside my skull is scarlet,
is your sunburn as you row. I drape you
with your white discarded shirt and brush
the grass into the lake. You ship the oars
and carefully you turn. We let the rowboat
drift into the mottled shade.

By night the loud black river charms you —
the cobbled path of cream it makes the moon.
You stargaze. I wish you wouldn't offer up
your throat to owls and ghosts. I urge you back,
close the cabin door, slide the beam
in place, and bank the little fire.

At our bedside in a thick white mug
the gentian's blue and closed in candlelight.
The bottle gentian's always closed.
Hers is the room of windows we come back to
finding bones among the blossoms. You pinch
the flame with two wet fingers.

EURYDICE

How could you forget me in the night?
Huddled speechless on the basement stairs
I know the dead live here, below the house.

Father, I am harmless as a mouse.
Who will dry my tears and braid my hair
if you forget your promise in the night?

Remember me and don't turn out the light.
At dinner, will my brother eat my share
while I am stranded here beneath the house?

Whatever dream or book you browse,
I cannot come to you except in prayer.
How could you forget me in the night?

Sweet milk turns to blood and fear to fright.
From boxes of what's broken creatures stare
who spend their midnight days below the house.

I beg you, up the tired darkness, rouse
yourself and bring me home into the light.
You never could forget me in the night
knowing, as you do, the dead beneath the house.

OVERHEARD ON THE RICHMOND FLOODWALL

Is it having seven siblings
that makes your face so private?
or is it that your father's Swiss?
Spare me Patrick Henry's church.
Your eyes are very blue.
No more Stonewall Jackson.
No more Arthur Ashe.
Outside the Cathedral of the Sacred Heart
I saw a falcon break a pigeon's neck.
Are you cruel or only shy?
Are you boring or only Swiss?
Above brown foam, steel struts,
and skyscrapers,
gulls full of poison
are choosing liberty and death.
No more history.
Let us cross the river
and lie among the trees.

VALENTINE'S NIGHT

I smooth the sofa's nap, changing velvet
from plum to red. My grandmother's banjo clock
strikes midnight early. You've slept so long
tonight, out cold since nine when we made love,
wishing for snow. The furnace thunders, waking.

On TV, a British scholar in designer jeans
sips espresso. I keep the volume low.
The daylight in Eleusis makes him squint.
Will it wake you, as he preaches proverbs
of rebirth? "You must face your death."
The camera pans away: an open coffin
holding someone's uncle. Noon flashes
off his wrist watch, children scatter dirt
like seed across his three-piece Sunday best.

I turn them off and creep upstairs and lean
above you, listening for breath.
If I woke you up, you'd find me crying.
All the time I waited for you — years
of months and hours — the future kept its distance.
North of here, my grandmother lies beneath
old snow and wisdom from Polonius.

The cave you've made in bed is warm. Feathers
of the *arbor vitae* stroke the glass,
drawing my attention to the snow.

IF YOU LIVED HERE, YOU'D BE HOME BY NOW

Driving home from the shore, we pass ripe acres
at 65, and then, within a moat
of Norway maples planted long ago
to mollify the wind, there is a farmhouse.
Horses nod in the barn beyond the aspen.
I know the mantle, too: willowware
full of zinnias on the varnished oak.
Gingham shirts and dresses ironed sharp
hang from the closet slant upstairs.
The tub has paws and guards a bathroom large
enough to pace. When the sun bears down,
we look for what needs doing in the shade.
When a storm rears up, the aspen silvers
and rain means even more than the house.

EAST BOOTH BAY

When a goblet tips,
the circle of wine on glass
becomes an oval.
Out there, the edge between
polished water and wrinkled water
is always shifting.

You tell me it's an eagle
in the nearest pine
but I shift the focus ring
to track the black eyestripe
of an osprey.

Dusk has a yellow edge.
Turn the mystery's page
and someone dies,
but grief is not the question
or the answer.

Each receding cloud
has a floor as strict as marble.
I nudge the glass
across the driftwood table.
If I push it over
what coastlines will it make?

Each tidal ripple
sharpens its pink crest
against black.
Over rocks you cannot see
the water swells against the air
as if it were a bodice.
The forest has teeth
and eats the sun.

SHOTS OF GARRETT COUNTY

Three scarlet maples
pose in the bleached high corn
of this one-horse field.

Black wings alight, there,
in the crooked one.

Treetops crowd the lake
crayon-yellow, berry, bronze,
snug as needlepoint.

Why did we come back?
Even here we cannot sleep
side by anxious side.

Down on Toothpick Road
apples ripen unobserved
in feral orchards.

A black bear stands up
still by the highway.

Clouds accumulate
all day. Accident, Mt. Savage,
and Luke — the towns are

mostly vertical.
Stone-rimmed eyes of empty shops
focus on the hills.

One thin cleft of woods
is drawn in frost, there.

We keep on driving.
I refold the map, suggest
a different route.

SNOW WHITE TURNS 39

I've been thinking how to break a talking mirror:
hammer and earplugs. Seven years of bad luck?
Peanuts, stacked against that Bette Davis
cackle, every morning when I hit the sink
without my make-up. One black dawn, I'll raise
my cheekbones to the light and all those watts
will fail to flush away these tear-track shadows.
Then I will smash the Glass. And take up chess.

No more clipping recipes for sautéed
hearts of virgin, I can tell you that,
or sending milkmaids out to feed the wolves.
No more wolves to feed, or woodsmen, either,
in our tidy kingdom. My husband found me
under glass. How I miss the woodsman.

WOODS HOLE

She talked about the flecks in his eyes, his flaxen
beard, the house in Maine, his classy backhand,
but the veteran my roommate loved was maimed:
he blanched, perhaps ashamed
to be alive, if they walked past someone's trash
in dark green plastic bags. Almost brash
ordinarily, then he couldn't talk
or drive. She'd gentle him along, they'd walk
and walk the beach till he snapped to. This role
was hard. And would she ever see him whole?
It made no sense to love him. That's what she said.
Back in Philadelphia that fall
she cried. And threw his letters out unread,
in a wicker basket down the hall.

EPIPHANY

Sweep the brittle needles out the door
and bleach the tired linen's greasy square.
The one who carved the bird carves here no more.

Lift the sash to January air.
What are you keeping all those ribbons for?
Plug in the iron. Press the linen square.

Make your resolution. Count the score
and let it fly — a metaphoric flare.
You'll never do his laundry anymore.

Trim your fingernails and cut your hair
into a shape that no one can ignore,
angled like a helmet, sharp and square.

Then sweep the headless partridge out the door,
the wingless angels, broken stars and pears,
and learn to sleep without the nagging snore

and in the morning at the grocery store
buy only what you like. No need to share.
Bleach the tired linen. Press it square.
The one who cut the tree cuts here no more.

DREAM SEQUENCE

The window boxes on the porch were full
of marigolds all summer. Now they're dead.
In my dream last night you said, "For God's sake,
pull them up and throw them out!" I did.

Then I dreamed my mother sat beside
a fire my father had laid. I was afraid
to find her dead but she woke up and smiled,
forgetting I had ever made her sad.

I don't remember how or why but once
I killed a lover, in a dream. (I've never
felt such guilt, awake.) But I don't inch
upon you with a knife, in sleep, or ever

dream you back, the way I do my parents,
for the comfort. You always come to nag.
My friends are trying not to say, Good riddance.
It's my line now — implying that I never begged

you not to leave, and if I take the blame,
no one knows. I'm bored by my "self-worth."
If I could choose my dreams, I'd wander home
and find you waiting, drowsy, by the hearth.

SEPTEMBER 10, 2001

Bless you, bagger of groceries,
    with your seven earrings
    and casual glaze.
Bless you, half-naked mower of lawns,
    quietly sweating,
    thoughtlessly smoking.
Old woman weeding tomatoes,
    bless your complaining back and knees
    and your unwatched tv.
Bless you, shingler of roofs,
    and bless your ordinary danger.
Bless you dog-walkers and postmen,
    you gossipers and nappers.
Bless you oblivious skate-boarders,
    without the sense to imagine a car.
Black cat, crooning for affection and food
    and nothing more,
    bless your ignorance.
Bless you, barn-red bungalow.
Bless your fire that clings to its pilot
    and its job at the tip of a match.
Bless you, toy plane in the sky,
    preparing to land an hour late
    amid the usual complaints.

GERTRUDE LANE NEWBERRY

My grandmother, 1874 — 1961

Our markers on the hill are not the same.
My sisters lived so long, their modern stones
are mirror smooth, with just the dates and names.
The baby twin died (leaving Jess alone)
some sixty years before. His is rough.
All that time and weather's rubbed away
whatever Mama asked the man to cut.
The other babies, too. But Dad would say,
"We count the living." A half mile down the hill
the brown Muskingum flows. Elsie liked
the thunder of the millrace, and the mill.
We were richer then, when Elsie died
at twelve: *Death Loves a Shining Mark.*
I read it with my fingers in the dark.

LANCASTRIAN LETTERS

After I saw Kenneth Branagh's remake of "Henry V" in 1990, I went back to see it four more times. Historical fiction set in medieval England had always been my escape-reading of choice, and I was at that time busy memorizing blank verse for an acting class every Saturday morning at the Washington Shakespeare Theatre. The mix of grit and poetry in the film sent me to the library for something like "the real story." There I found Desmond Seward's *Henry V, The Scourge of God*. It was Seward, Branagh, and Shakespeare who suggested to me that there were stories still to tell about Henry V, voices still to be heard.

WHITSUNDAY, 1394: MARY DE BOHUN
wife of Henry Bolingbroke, Earl of Derby,
to Joan, Countess of Hereford.

Don't be angry, Mother. I did it all,
Joanna made the pennyroyal tea,
but nothing worked. The baby's kicking now,
I can't bear to wish it otherwise.
I wonder when you came to change of life?

Finally this year, your roses flourish.
I keep some, pale and cool, beside my bed
all day. Henry sets one by his music.
Even little Blanche grows still, smiling
as she noses at her namesake blossoms.

The boys, however, threaten them each day.
I heard them in the garden Tuesday morning,
Thomas boasting he could shoot his water
farthest. Harry wouldn't try — and wisely.
(Yes, he's older then Tom, and taller, too,
but hasn't so large a member.) Thomas hit him,
as Harry hoped he would, or so I think,
for Harry never loses in a fight.
Humphrey cheered for Tom, John for Harry,
and I, nearly sick at the window, for the roses.
Growing up a sister to a sister
is no training for this motherhood.

Mother, come soon. My back hurts all the time now.
My stillborn baby's often in my thoughts.
Was I twelve? You came and took me home
from being Henry's little wife, ashamed
and so relieved to be a child again.

JULY 3, 1395: JOAN, COUNTESS OF HEREFORD
to her son-in-law Henry, Earl of Derby
and son of the Duke of Lancaster.

Young Harry's ill again, the bloody flux
and likely mortal, though Dr. Pye has hopes.
The other brothers lurk about the hall
watching chamberpots and filthy linen
trundled in and out, struck too dumb
to thrash each other for their hearts' relief.
Since Mary died last summer, and Harry seems
to follow now, they've worked it out
they all will die by 1400, one girl
or boy each year until the century's end.
Prying splinters from their grubby fingers
I discovered they are building coffins
for each other. I have never seen
a child go mad. For their peace and Harry's
I've packed them off to Kenilworth.
The girls, of course, are not a problem.

APRIL 15, 1399: HENRY BOLINGBROKE
to his mother-in-law Joan, from exile in France.

The spring is fine in Paris, where I'm honored
as I should be, though my debts increase.
Any sum you raise — for ships or soldiers
to bring me home to my inheritance —
will keep your grandsons rich. I know, of course,
King Richard's off to Ireland, with Harry, hostage.
Richard hasn't got the nerve or wit
to deal with Ireland ... an education, though,
for Harry. I hear they're fond of one another.
In any case, I have me three more sons.
Don't breed the greyhound bitch until I come.

OCTOBER 13, 1399: THE BISHOP OF WINCHESTER
to the Duke of Exeter (both half-brothers of
Bolingbroke).

At last our brother's king, and we shall rise.
(Cousin Richard's tucked up in the Tower.)
The coronation, with all our brawling nephews
stroking their new weapons, was resplendent.
I only wish that Bolingbroke had washed
his hair. The lice were not a happy omen.

PENTECOST, 1401: HENRY, PRINCE OF WALES (1387-1422), to his brother John, Duke of Bedford.

Conwy fell last week. Nine Welsh traitors
spent Good Friday losing guts and balls,
speaking in tongues and glad to lose their heads.
Even before they've been fileted, they stink.
The girls are sweet, though — Worcester has them bathed.
Father sent new cannon. You can't believe
what single gunstones do in these old forts.
But he will not send enough to pay my men.

TWELFTH NIGHT, 1403: BLANCHE
(1392-1406), daughter of Henry IV (Bolingbroke)
and wife of Louis of Bavaria, to her sister Philippa.

I think it's wonderful to be a princess
though Father was more easy with his gold
before. All the food here's creamy sweet!
Louis likes me fat and so I am.
We love each other very much except
he said that Father had King Richard killed.
I hit him with my doll but he went on,
"That's what great men do. You should be proud!"
so I forgave him, but I write to say
that Father said King Richard starved himself
to death. (I could not starve myself a little.)
I liked King Richard — I mean, Cousin Richard —
he gave me that nice spaniel, Harry liked him, too.
All that time in Ireland, he told me once,
the King was like a father to him. I suppose
that someone very good could starve himself
to death. But ask John. Not Harry, who says
what must be said, but John, who'll tell the truth.

JULY 22, 1403: HENRY, PRINCE OF WALES
and son of Henry IV (Bolingbroke), makes his
confession after the Battle of Shrewsbury.

Forgive me, Father, for I have sinned:
eleven archers dead and twenty knights,
more I think than His Grace, my father, killed.

And during Mass, before we marched, my thoughts
were of the girl who hid in the standing corn
when we took Conwy, the things we did with her.

And I dreamed the dream again. King Richard —
it must be Richard's ghost — he smiles at me,
I play my harp for him, he calls me "gallant."

And I was angry with His Grace. My father
sent no pay all spring, he makes me out
a fool. I sell my plate to pay my troops.

But mainly this: when I saw them gathered
in their thousands above us on the ridge,
every bowman wearing Richard's badge,
and all the Bullfeld laid out rising green
between us, shining ponds still thin and clear,
the heavy crop of summer peas still standing,
and suddenly the whine and needle shadows
of their arrows, one that slices me
from mouth to ear — then I saw God's back.

Before we took the hill, my open cheek
scabbing to the inside of my helmet,
I was sure the arrow came from Richard
up in Heaven, and we were damned. For these,
and all my sins, I am most heartily sorry.

ALL SAINTS' DAY, 1406: PHILIPPA (1394-1430), Queen of Denmark, Norway, and Sweden, to her brother John, Duke of Bedford.

Missing Blanche and jealous of her baby,
I received the lad that brought the news.
Is it a rule? If you are happy, you
die young? Her boy survives, so I'm still jealous,
wicked as the sisters in the tale.

Remember how you rescued me from Thomas?
Rescue me again. You can't imagine:
there's scarcely daylight in the winter here.
Please make Father ask me home to visit.
My husband will not mind, nor want to come.

MARCH 21, 1413: HENRY V
makes his confession after
the death of his father, Henry IV.

"What right have *you* to the crown, since I have none?"
He never spoke these words aloud before,
or even thought them. So I would have sworn.
How many men have died so he could wear it?
"I'll keep it as you took it, by the sword."
This turned his mind to France. But he was dying
and I was glad. And still am glad.
For this, and all my sins, may God forgive me.

PASSION SUNDAY, 1413: THOMAS (1388-1421), Duke of Clarence and brother of Henry V, to his brother-in-law Eric, King of Denmark, Norway, and Sweden.

How can I thank you for the sword?
A finer steel than any I have held.
Today I wore it to the coronation —
in the snow! The country's in a blizzard
such as we have never seen in April
(though it would hardly keep a Dane at home).
Many men and animals have died.
Harry was grim, expecting, I suppose,
more auspicious weather from the Lord.

SEPTEMBER 2, 1414: JOHN
(1389-1435), Duke of Bedford and brother of the king, to his uncle, the Duke of Exeter.

Courtenay's off to Paris, smiling peace:
Harry asks for all of western France,
two million crowns, and Princess Catherine.
Meanwhile the gunstones multiply in London.
They count out rams and ladders in Southampton,
ropes and chains and calthrops, picks and shovels.
While you're in Chester, see about more bows.

JUNE 30, 1415: THE BISHOP
of Winchester to his brother, the Duke of Exeter.

This is bracing work. Yesterday
the French archbishop scolded young King Henry
(and he all decked in cloth of gold):
"Regarding land to which you claim the right,
you have no lordship, not even England,
which by right belongs to Richard's heir,
the Earl of March, a man of peace and honor."
Henry stormed out, all rustling light —
not often now you see him in a temper.
I find it charming. He's marked the old man down
for something special, once we are in France.

NOVEMBER 11, 1415: HUMPHREY
(1391-1447), Duke of Gloucester and youngest brother of the king, to his brother John, Duke of Bedford.

Thanks for your concern. I'm knitting well.
Though still unable to sit or ride, I read,
lying on my belly by the fire.
A pity you and Thomas were not there
at Agincourt — French piled up as high
as Holland dikes. Thus God affirms the just.
I found a splendid missal at Harfleur
in the ashes of the parish church.

CHRISTMAS, 1418: JOAN, COUNTESS
of Hereford, to Henry V, her grandson.

I pray the people of Rouen will see
the justice of your siege and yield.
Eating dogs and cats and rats and roots ...
But, heartless burghers! to turn the peasants out,
where they are caught between our English arrows
and the wrong side of the Norman walls!
Beware of plague — they rot so near you
in the ditch. Keep warm, and Happy Christmas!
Drink only wine and never touch the pork.

MARCH 11, 1421: CATHERINE OF VALOIS
(1401-1437), princess of France and bride
of Henry V, to her sister, Marie.

Of course, he's English, but King, after all,
and so clean! As soon as Mother learned
he wanted me, I was fitted for a gown,
my first new gown in two years, and given eggs
and butter with my piece of bread each morning.
Henry always brings me marzipan.

But anything is better than the days
we spent locked up on one side of the hall,
Father locked up screaming on the other.
No one cared if we ate or not. And younger nights,
remember? Awake and cold by Mother's bed
while she played with Orleans? I hate
to lie alone, even now. Who's to say
we're father's children, any of us?

But Harry, my St. George, has never questioned.
I love the heated baths, the cherry velvet,
the groaning golden plates, and my husband.
I even love his handsome battle scar.
(The Flemish painter did not dare to draw it.)
At my coronation, it being Lent,
they served us more than twenty kinds of fish!
The best was conger, drowned in almond cream.
Come and visit me, we'll eat and eat!

GOOD FRIDAY, 1421: THOMAS, DUKE
of Clarence harangues his bastard son.

Do not distress yourself about the odds.
They're mostly French and, even with their Scots,
no match for English cavalry.
The King's away, I'm in charge in France,
and you, my son, have not spent half your life
explaining why you weren't at Agincourt,
October twenty-fifth, the-Bleeding-Year-
of-Our-Bleeding-Lord, 1415.
(Have you cleaned my Italian scabbard yet?)
His Grace your uncle's famous for his nerve
but Agincourt was all topography
and mud. (No, not like that, you'll scratch
the silver.) I know my brother's careful ass.
He won't move off the pot without his archers.
When minstrels have forgotten Agincourt,
they'll sing about Baugé and valiant Clarence,
the uncrowned Lionheart of this dark age.
(Boar bristle's what you need to loosen blood
from where it's hardened down between the roses.)

APRIL 1, 1421: HENRY V
to a survivor of the Battle of Baugé.

One hundred fifty against five thousand?
My grief is greatly tempered by my anger.
Never give battle without archers.
How can I proceed with half my captains
wounded, dead, or captive? If he had lived,
I would have had my brother to the block
for insubordination. I am in earnest.
I trust he knows, in Hell, it was bowmen
dragged his body from the field of honor.

JULY 21, 1422: JOHN, DUKE OF BEDFORD,
to the Duke of Burgundy,
ally of the English in France.

We are dispatching archers up the Loire
to you at Cosne but the King will stay
in Paris. He is a little weary, uneasy
in the gut. It plagues him in the heat.
Be confident, as he is, of success,
attended by his spirit and his bowmen.

SEPTEMBER 1, 1422: JOHN, DUKE OF BEDFORD,
to his sister Philippa, Queen
of Denmark, Norway, and Sweden.

Harry died last night. Bedford and Exeter,
Warwick and Talbot — we drift about Vincennes
like orphans, wondering how we came to France.
He had been weakening all summer, in the way
that he was sick when we were little children.
Then, at Charenton, he swung up in the saddle
and collapsed across the reins. From his bed
he spent ten days dispensing France and England.
I'm thankful Tom died first and never knew
that Harry left him nothing in his will.

SEPTEMBER 15, 1422: THE DUKE OF EXETER
to his brother, the Bishop of Winchester.

There's no truth to it. His confidence
in the French enterprise was firm, even
at the end. Perhaps a glimpse of Hell
sent as a final trial — "You lie!" he cried,
delirious, "my portion lies with Christ!"
But then slipped off in shriven peace.
I never fought beside a better man.
Nothing must be written of that scar
across his cheek he got at Shrewsbury.
Twice he pressed me on this, like a girl.

JUNE 2, 1430: CATHERINE OF VALOIS
remembers her first husband on the tenth
anniversary of their wedding.

He was kind and generous, sleek
to touch and look at, always late to bed
and early gone. When his baby came,
I lay in at Windsor. He stayed in Paris.

Even dying, he didn't send for me,
though we'd been apart eleven months.
Not so clean at the end and always vain.
You cannot guess what it was like, like God
had died again. English or French, no one
thought he could — die. I wept until
my breastbones hurt, my eyelids stiff as paper.
All that fall I rode behind a coffin
filled with Henry's bones, boiled clean. Town
by town, we rode: Rouen, Montreuil, Boulogne,
Calais; then Dover, Canterbury, London.

But I cannot bear to lie alone,
hearing my mother's lovers in the curtains,
wondering if there will be dawn or breakfast.
So, after Henry died, despite his brothers,
I married with my handsome servant Tudor.
He likes to lie abed and keep me warm.
Our children have amusing dreams
and do not fear the dark. (My son the Prince
repeats his beads more often than he eats.
His darting eyes remind me of my father's.)

But Owen Tudor's eyes are black and merry.
I have it written down we'll lie together
when we die. I look for no more time
with Henry up in Heaven than in France.
There is no marzipan in Paradise
(so my confessor claims). Perhaps. But I,
at least, shall have a husband. I shall not spend
forever lying lonely in the dark.

AUGUST 31, 1435: JOHN, DUKE OF BEDFORD, prays for his brother Henry's soul.

Thirteen years I've born his torch for France
alone, but still I smell it in my sleep.
It wakes me grunting. I turn and stick my nose
into the linen, surely something dead
is burning in the pillow. But no. She stands
beside the candle — the headless girl at Caen,
her child still sucking. Harry puked — and stopped
the killing. He did Your Work with dedication:
all those masses, all those dying babies
baptized in the ditch outside Rouen.
But who is it, burning in my dreams?
"War without fire is like sausages
without mustard," says Harry in the night.
Kyrie eleison. Christe eleison.

HALLOWE'EN, 1437: HUMPHREY,
Duke of Gloucester, to Henry V's biographer

I tremble for my books in this long rain.
I lay them out wide open near the fire
and turn the pages one by one throughout
the day to keep them separate and dry.
Nothing grieves me like a moldy book.
Henry's library was large, though not
so large, I think, as mine.

Many thanks
for this new handsome *Vita*. As you note,
my brothers John and Thomas did not fight
at Agincourt. I trace all my misfortune
to their envy. If I had had a son ...
We were not lucky in our making children,
one legitimate heir between us four
and he, insane. I wish the rain would stop.

I was there at Shrewsbury, you know,
though only twelve. Did I neglect to mention
Henry was knighted twice? Once of course
by Father. Once by Richard, in darkest Ireland.

MAY 21, 1471: HENRY VI
(1421-1471), in the Tower, to his wife, a fugitive
in France, upon hearing of the death of their only child.

Margaret, I cannot keep the paper dry.
As well you are not here to watch me weep.
I see you scowling. And remember him
as if he were my father's son, not mine,
so alike they were, by all accounts —
brisk and clever warriors. Was I
ambassador, a kind of Gabriel,
to join his seed to your ferocious heart?

Thank God you're safe. I am oddly calm,
splendidly, boringly, sane. I love these tears:
any father's grieving tears. My guard
delivers skins of sour Rhenish, trading
them for prayers. He says I will be sainted.
He thinks I do not know I will be martyred.

The nights are warmer now, my sleep improves.
Do you remember the April day we met?
You thought I was more handsome than my picture
before you knew about my fragile wits.
Whatever broke between us, he was my son.
Believe that I believe it. And both forgive.

Someone's on the stair. My wine steward,
no doubt. I'll end this. God keep you in His Hand
as I keep you in my heart. Henry.

OTHER PRINCES

THE COMMON CUP

Little mention's made of other grails:
the gourd the woman gave him at the well,
the goblet he was handed at the wedding,
the amphora he filled there.
Did Peter's mother use the bowl again
once Jesus made her well enough to cook?
Perhaps he stroked the rim with a calloused thumb
and scooped his fill of dinner with a shard
of broken bread. Martha kept a cup
for him and him alone in Bethany.
The alabaster jar was meant to break ...
and all are broken now, and more than broken,
especially the ones without a story.
Was that rough chalice chipped? The earthenware
he drank from in his mother's house in Nazareth
when he came home with sawdust in his throat?

UP IN THE OLD HOTEL

Still acquiring pieces of the man
he needs to be, he bought it hardback.
Once a journalist, he imagines
Mitchell might have been a mentor,
the author's barren decades
only another cause for bonding.

He likes his fiction hardback, too,
and guns, expensive pipes, fishing rods
and recurve bows. All are timber
and thatch the child has built
the man he fathered.
They shelter there against a storm
of bosses, women, voices of the dead
and crazy, Prozac be damned.

"I never had a childhood,"
he tells his handsome son
whose gift, *American Psycho,*
lies beneath the lighted tree.
"I'm still thirteen." No one bothers
to point out the inconsistency
but the boy remarks,
"I guess that leaves me out,"
and goes on wrecking cars and girls,
determined to be at least another beam
in his father's weeping eye.

HERO-SURFING

Black jerseys over black t-shirts
are this young pitcher's luck
in the 99 degree night,
but the team is only losing drenched
since they pulled him after six.
The catcher throws a runner out.
It won't change the outcome.
Cameras catch the shine
of sweaty ringlets on his neck.

... Dropping names, rehearsing scandals,
the neatly-bearded poet warms
the screen with his smile.
Discussing his poems on camera
in a cluster of women —
it's a sixth sense. He's proud
of his trim shirt,
of all the trees he's loved,
of breaking his lines after "the."

... They're still losing in the ninth
but the shortstop dives and rises
(6 to 4 to 3) and in the bottom
the catcher hits a long drive into right
but slides into third too late,
splitting his lip.
In the damp black cotton of pride
and failed luck,
he won't go home tonight.

THE PRINCE WHO WOKE BRIAR ROSE

He talked too much, according to the king.
She, however, knew the prince's blather
for the outward audible sign of waking life.
And she was no angel, either, with a cold
knot left in her heart from so much sleep; and
from spending all her life where nothing's spun.

But somehow she grew up, asleep, and knew
the nervous prince for what he was.
For him, the hedge of thorn trees parted.
She didn't see the crimson brambles shrink
away like spiny creatures of the deep,
or all the other princes moldering —
athletes, statesmen. Was he the better man?
He knew enough to keep on walking and find
the winding tower stairs. There she lay.

For his unspeaking mouth, she opened wide
her eyes. Or was it more than just a kiss?
the shaking of the bed? The prince for once
voracious? Pushing, missing, finally home?
Whatever. They were married after lunch.

Married now twelve years, king for three,
he still can't take his status in. At banquets,
he talks of how it feels to be the Hero;
describes the sleepers in the quiet hall:
the cook with greasy spoon upraised to strike
the scullion, the cocker spaniel poised to scratch,
the manicurist and the queen. Cobwebs?
No worse than you'd expect in any castle.
All the spiders slept, as well.

She studies, while he talks, the borderland
beneath his chin where beard begins and where
it deepens. He is her unenchanted land,
the woods and hills and gullies of the world
she missed those hundred dateless springs.

She sleeps a different sleep beside her prince
from which, for certain years and days, she'll wake
each ordinary morning to a whiff
of coffee, briefly fresh; the ticking clock;
a splash of moving sun across the panes.

MAELBRIGTE'S WOMAN

Orkneyinga Saga, chapter 5

Near nine hundred years
since the White Christ and still
the world goes on, dark and wintered.
If my husband's life was short and brutish,
what is it worth the time to say
about my own? We were ignorant of much
but not of anything that kills.

None of Earl Sigurd's men were clever,
even Aud "the Deep Minded,"
a great drunken skraeling with brains
in his sea-legs only. But they took it all,
Caithness to Ross,
and angled for the lowlands
which we held, Maelbrigte and I,
with blood and wit and healthy sons.
Earl Sigurd sent a herald south
asking parley, to settle boundaries,
each chieftain to be backed by forty horse.
Maelbrigte agreed.

"Will you go with only forty men?"
I kissed his little crooked dogtooth
and snuggled close, smelling the ghost
of the bear who kept us warm.

"Forty is my bond, my honor."

"How many men, do you suppose,
will be enough to bind up Sigurd's honor?"

"Hush. A good soft wife would take
my mind away from Sigurd." So I did,
as best I might.

The bards relate that Sigurd thought
the bargain forty *horses*, not forty warriors.
He came south with two men
mounted on each pony.

All our host were dead by noon
(and many more than forty
from Caithness).
They took the Scottish heads
to cure and carry home to Norway
in the spring. Sigurd himself
strung leather through my husband's brain.
Slung grimacing behind the great earl's saddle,
Maelbrigte bumped and snagged
and tore the victor's leg
all twelve miles to Thurso.

Sigurd the Powerful took nine days dying.
He is buried where the badgers go to piss.
My eldest son has brought me home
his father's head. I have not asked him
how or what or who it cost
but I have used it in a charm.
During Lent last month,
Sigurd's only son died of rancid eel
and left no child.

And still we hold the border.
And still I go to bed at night alone
as if the morning were a promise
I desired to keep. And still
I kiss the crooked tooth
when nothing else will bring me sleep.

HALLGERD'S BOWSTRING
Reading *Njal's Saga*

1. The Farmers

Here in Iceland, small, volcanic jewel,
the names of men alone may be a sign.
The year is 1011, nearing Yule.
The Althing's over. Men begin to shine
the weapons which their love of law denied
them back in June. They will cleave your skull
without much forethought in the eventide
and then engage both witnesses and counsel
before the Dog Star rises. Women speak
only to urge their sons to shed more blood
for honor's sake. If they cook or weep,
we are not told. Are the bodies in the mud
meant to make us passionate for glory?
No answers on the skin that tells the story.

2. Itinerant Hags

If answers on the skin that tells the story
could name these three old women who appear
in threadbare wool, would it change your quarry?
Would you take the road they point to? Are they seers?
They don't pretend to magic. They saw the men
you hate while walking out along the barrens.
If the storyteller knows they're sent
by Death to guarantee he gets his share and
if at home they do not dine in rags,
he doesn't say. They come when needed, plodding
tirelessly along Rang River, bags
stitched up with runes, eyes filmed-over, bodies
bent, for now, as if with grief and chance.
Later in their ribbons they will dance.

3. The Woman

Hallgerd, in her ribbons, loves to dance.
She's probably their equal in sheer malice
and in will. A husband should enhance
one's joy, and joy to fill the empty chalice.
If he slaps his goddess (and all three will),
her foster father Thjostolf will avenge
the hurt. Twice for Hallgerd he will kill.
(I wonder if they're more than kin and friends.)
Thjostolf has this one redeeming trait:
he seems to love her. Otherwise he's scum.
A grieving Hallgerd sends him to his fate
the windy day he whets his axe on one
she loves. But, used to murder for her sake,
he found the loyal habit hard to break.

4. The Names

Puzzlement's a feeling hard to shake
even after ninety chapters. Bork
Bluetooth-Beard? Flosi? Sigurd-the-Snake-
in-the-Eye? Gizur the White, Ketil of Mork?
"Gunnar" and "Njal" are not so strange
and "Mord" is just the evil name you'd give him.
But, like a scribbled margin on each page,
they bring the oddity of truth. Asgrim
as what? Brynjolf Unruly? As grim as Thrain?
Or Hallbjorn the Strong? As grim as him?
Skarp-Hedin, Starkad: sharp enough to maim.
But Gunnar's hound was just called "Sam." Slim
and fierce, he would have saved his master's life —
but died beneath Onund of Trollwood's knife.

5. The Death of Gunnar

The night's made quiet by the Trollwood's knife
but Gunnar sees his enemies and with his bow
kills two and wounds another eight. His life,
though it seemed charmed against defeat till now,
at last depends upon a new bowstring.
Though Hallgerd loves his sure and gentle touch,
he slapped her once, returning from the Althing
(she'd proved a thief). She loves, but not as much
as she needs to wield her slender power.
He wounds eight more attackers, with no bow,
is killed at last. As these new widowed hours
pass, becoming years, does she even know
what's lost? Does she blame herself or care?
His wife refused him just two locks of hair.

6. The Ghost of Gunnar

Hallgerd refused him just two locks of hair
to bind up life. Gunnar, entombed upright,
awakes and sings and doesn't seem to care.
He terrifies the countryside all night
with his delight at never having given in.
The mound is lit by four unearthly torches
and verses heard afar, from deep within.
His mother keeps his halberd, though it scorches,
waiting for the one who'll use it right.
Hogni sees his father's ghost, and hears
his father's anger is immortal. Unlike
Hamlet, feeling neither doubt nor fear,
he takes the halberd. Like a beast, it lows —
and murders twice before the rooster crows.

7. The Burning of Njal

Murder celebrates each rooster crow,
it seems, and reaches Gunnar's friend, Njal,
at last. He's quite unlike the others — no
ferocity, no beard. Call him "Neil."
He looks familiar. He can't start a fight
or keep himself from trying to make peace,
however awkward. The lawful costly Right
is for him a kind of Golden Fleece.
He pays for it with silver; and with the pain
of seeing what's to come; of shielding ones
who bruise him everytime they speak; of laying
down with his old wife and young grandson
in bed, to wait for fire to do it's cruel
work, in Iceland — small, volcanic jewel.

TURF-EINAR

Orkneyinga Saga, chapters 6 - 8

1. *A Slice From the Family Shield*

Rognvald of More had sons enough
for each day of the week
(discounting Sunday, province of the Christ).
He lost a son to cowardice,
another son to Normandy.
Then he went a'viking with King Harald
and gave a third to Death.

He had another gift to give:
the Orkneys — and the work
of driving off two Danes who rampaged there.
To the eldest son remaining he remarked,
"Your path is not the swanroad."
To the middle, "You're bound for Iceland."
The youngest, a one-eyed bastard,
spoke up out of turn:

"Give me the islands
and I'll give your heart's desire:
you won't see me again."

"You? And your mother slave-born
on both sides? Though you're wise enough
in this: nothing would cheer me
like seeing the back of you for good."

He gave the boy a ship of twenty benches
and wrote a letter to King Harald
who made young Einar Earl of Orkney.

But what Einar's remembered for
is digging peat for fuel at Tarbat Ness.
No one had thought of it till then,
and a bright idea it was,
on a cold and treeless strand.

2. *Turf-Einar Gave Tree-Beard to the Trolls*

Einar had no trouble getting men
to fill his twenty benches
and kill the Danes
(Thorir Tree-Beard and Kalf Scurvy)
who thought they ruled his islands.
He slid their bodies overboard
and spoke a couplet in their memory.

3. *Not From My Brother's Hand, the Hurled Shaft*

How did Einar lose that eye?
It can't be hard to make
your little brother prove his nerve
(like the son of William Tell did)
when you both know
your father hates the little bastard.

4. *Our Duty is to the Dead*

King Harald back in Norway
also had a son that made his father cringe.
"Halfdan Longleg," he was called.
He murdered Einar's father
and called himself the Earl of Shetland.

Einar sailed for Scots to man his ships
and then returned to harry Halfdan
off the coast of Hoy.
When the prince jumped overboard
Einar hauled him back,
laid him on the deck,
pruned the ribs from off his spine
and harvested his lungs
through these new mouths.

Then Einar offered up
the Prince of Norway's blood to Odin
and, as the moon was full,
he made a poem.
It felt so good between his teeth,
he spoke another.

On Hoxa, heaving stones with all his crew,
Einar piled a cairn on Halfdan Lungless.
It rose within a blaze of summer heather.
Sweat pouring down the swag of flesh
that was his wounded eye,
Einar made a poem.

5. *Sweetly the Norns*

When Harald's other sons
heard about their brother
(short of breath) they shouted
drunken threats against Turf-Einar.
The King of Norway told them
what their chances were and boxed their ears
in front of all his guests from Rome.

Drinking beer beside the fire,
Einar heard the story after dinner.
In his snuggest farmhouse
on the prow of Egilsay,
he squeezed his pretty wife
and put his flagon down
and made a poem.
Everybody listened.

AUDITIONS FOR "HAMLET" AT THE UNITARIAN CHURCH

I can hardly say how much I wanted
to be chosen "Gertrude," to go ahead
and just be middle-aged, not beautiful
but not too bad, and with so many lines.

The Queen's cerebral, cranky son
should have a family of his own by now
and she's embarrassed: he's thirty, overweight,
unmarried, and so easy to supplant.
Besides, this second love is sweet —
and how it might have come about is easy
not to ponder. She loved the elder Hamlet
and, after all, he doesn't feel the need
to haunt her nights, so who is Hamlet Jr.
to clock her grief and say she ought to miss
the man who shielded her from heaven's wind?

Though she gets pushed around and yelled at,
it's all *onstage.* It would be good enough
to play the Player Queen, even a man,
even Francisco, with eight bare lines, among them:
"'Tis bitter cold and I am sick at heart."

But Gertrude gets to tell about Ophelia
and the nettles. (Nettles are how you know
the girl is really nuts.) Gertrude cares
as Hamlet never does. Obedient
Ophelia might have made it all okay —
or might have taken with her down the brook
the only grandchild of the Queen.
Gertrude breaks the news as if she felt
it *needed* to be done in poetry
and, grasping for a different ending, she takes
Laertes' hand ... and finally the cup,
loving both her son and second husband,
though they have never failed to take her life.

THE LAST BREAKFAST

> *This was now the third time that Jesus revealed himself to the disciples after he was raised from the dead.* John 21:14

The black spine of the dory
barely wavers against the red east.
He can count his seven friends —
Nathanael's skinny elbows at an angle
with the lifted oars;
Peter poised to dive into the net;
and John, too young to be worn out
by a night of fishing or of loss,
waving at the sky as if
to rhapsodize the bloody dawn.

It's cold.
The pebbles hurt his feet.
He'll miss his feet
and miss their hurting, too,
but he smiles, imagining
the faces of his friends
as they inhale the toasting
flatbread and the fish.

No more campfires after this
or loaves and fishes,
but this last is bread from heaven
and trout from the stream
that ripples by the throne.
And why not coffee from the future?
The galvanized pot
is streaked with galaxies.

The water boils.
The fish skin crackles.
It gives him so much pleasure
to make their breakfast
that they blur in his eyes as they labor.

Surely they will smell the fish and turn.
But they are comfortable, comforted,
in Simon Peter's old skiff.
The hungry fragrance travels.
Surely they will smell the coffee and turn.
How far he's come to make their coffee.
Surely he won't be forced
to work another miracle.
Surely, surely, they will turn.

Anne Sheldon was born in Washington, DC, and graduated from Swarthmore College. Formerly a children's librarian, she lives in Silver Spring, Maryland, with two cats, where she is active in her church. She is currently a poet-in-the-schools working through the Maryland State Arts Council and teaches storytelling at the College of Library and Information Sciences at the University of Maryland. As a storyteller, she has performed widely in the mid-Atlantic region. Her repertoire includes folktales and legends as well as her own narrative poetry and that of classic poets such as Robert Frost.

Photograph by Adrian Verkouteren